Collins

AMAZING PLAC

FASCINATING FACTS

Published by Collins
An imprint of HarperCollins Publishers
Westerhill Road
Bishopbriggs
Glasgow G64 2QT
www.harpercollins.co.uk

First published 2013
Second edition 2016

A catalogue record for this book is available from the British Library

ISBN 978-0-00-816919-0

10 9 8 7 6 5 4 3

Printed in Hong Kong by Printing Express Ltd.

All mapping in this book is generated from Collins Bartholomew
digital databases.
Collins Bartholomew, the UK's leading independent geographical
information supplier, can provide a digital, custom, and premium
mapping service to a variety of markets.
For further information:
Tel: +44 (0)208 307 4515
e-mail: collinsbartholomew@harpercollins.co.uk
Visit our website at: www.collins.co.uk www.collinsbartholomew.com

If you would like to comment on any aspect of this book, please
contact us at the above address or online.
e-mail: collinsmaps@harpercollins.co.uk

Contents

The Seven Ancient Wonders

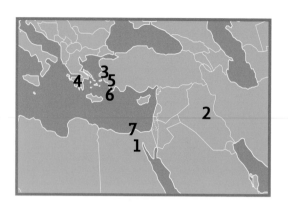

The Seven Wonders of the Ancient World were the architectural and artistic monuments considered to be perfect by the Greeks and the Romans. Most of the original ancient wonders no longer exist. Today, the Great Pyramid of Giza is the only wonder still standing.

1. Great Pyramid of Giza
The most ancient and the only survivor of the original Seven Wonders of the Ancient World, the Great Pyramid of Giza, also called Pyramid of Khufu, is located near the city of Cairo, in Egypt.

2. Hanging Gardens of Babylon
There is some doubt over the existence of this ancient wonder and no record of when it was built. However it is thought that King Nebuchadnezzar built the gardens in Babylon's flat desert landscape to please his wife.

3. Temple of Artemis at Ephesus
The Temple of Artemis was one of the most elegant buildings of ancient times. Located in Turkey, 50 km (30 miles) south of the city of Izmir, it was destroyed and re-built several times between 600 BC and AD 262.

4. Statue of Zeus at Olympia

This colossal statue represented the Greek god of heaven: Zeus. It was created by a famous Greek sculptor called Phidias. It was destroyed during a fire which ravaged the temple in AD 462 and today only the stony ruins which were used for the construction of the temple remain.

5. Mausoleum at Halicarnassus

The Mausoleum at Halicarnassus, an enormous grave built in the 4th century for King Mausolus, was located in southwest Turkey in the city of Halicarnassus (now known as Bodrum).

6. Colossus of Rhodes

It took twelve years of hard work to build the bronze statue honouring the Greek sun god Helios. This statue, known as The Colossus of Rhodes, was built around 280 BC and could easily be seen by ships approaching the harbour. It was partially destroyed by an earthquake in 225 BC.

7. Lighthouse of Alexandria

This is one of the best known of all the ancient monuments. The Lighthouse was located in Egypt on the island of Pharos in front of the city of Alexandria. The lighthouse, made of white marble, had three floors, one square, one octagonal and the third cylindrical.

Great Pyramid of Giza

There are three pyramids at Giza. They are far bigger than most people would imagine. Even more amazing is the fact that they were built nearly 4600 years ago and are still standing today.

The Great Pyramid of Giza (also known as the Pyramid of Khufu) is the oldest and largest of the three pyramids. It is truly an astonishing work of engineering skill and for over four thousand years, until modern times, it was the tallest building in the world. It is the oldest of the Seven Wonders of the Ancient World and the only one to remain largely intact. It was built using over two million limestone blocks, which were then cased in smooth limestone.

Africa

Africa

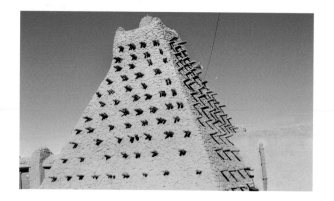

1. Timbuktu, Mali
The city of Timbuktu grew rich as a stopping point for travelling merchants. It also became famous as a Muslim holy place and centre of learning. Timbuktu's mosques were part of a cultural Golden Age in the 15th and 16th centuries. Mosques were built using mud bricks. Many of these mosques survive in their original form to this day.

2. Sahara Desert
The Sahara Desert is the world's hottest desert. There are frequent sandstorms. The Sahara covers most of North Africa, stretching 5000 km (3000 miles) across and up to 2000 km (1200 miles) from head to foot. The United States of America or China could fit into it. Some of its sand dunes are 180 m (590 ft) high.

3. Marrakesh, Morocco
The elegant Koutoubia minaret is Marrakesh's most famous landmark. The tower stands 77 m (253 ft) high and is part of the biggest mosque in the city. It watches over the Jemaa El Fna souk, or open-air marketplace. The minaret was built over 800 years ago.

4. Karnak, Egypt

The Temple of Karnak in Luxor is an incredible complex of chapels, gateways, obelisks, pillars and carvings. It was built over a period of 1500 years from 2800 BC and was the ancient Egyptians' most sacred place. Karnak is huge – the world's three largest cathedrals combined would fit into it. One of its ancient obelisks is the tallest on earth, standing 29.6 m (97 ft) high.

5. Abu Simbel, Egypt

The twin temples at Abu Simbel were carved out of a mountainside in the 13th century BC. The Great Temple is famous for its four colossal statues of the Pharaoh Rameses II. These guard the temple's entrance. The Small Temple also has large rock-cut figures. Both temples were moved in 1968 to avoid being flooded when the Aswan High Dam was built on the nearby River Nile.

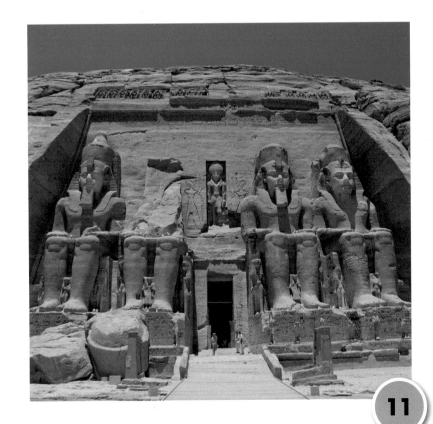

Africa

1. Kilimanjaro, Tanzania
Kilimanjaro is a spectacular volcanic mountain in Tanzania. It is the highest mountain in Africa at 5892 m (19 331 ft). It is dormant, and last erupted 150 000 years ago. But there are active fumaroles (small vents that belch gas) in its crater and the mountain could erupt again. Kilimanjaro's summit was once completely covered by an ice cap with glaciers. This ice field has been shrinking in the last 100 years and will probably disappear completely.

2. Serengeti, Tanzania and Kenya
The greatest animal show on earth happens every year on the Serengeti Plains in Tanzania and Kenya. As seasonal rains begin to fall, millions of animals migrate to find the newly ripened grass. Around 750 000 zebra and 1.2 million wildebeest make the dangerous journey every year. Many die of hunger, exhaustion or fall prey to hungry lions.

3. Ngorongoro Crater, Tanzania
The Ngorongoro volcano was one of the world's tallest mountains 3 million years ago. Then it blew itself apart in a catastrophic explosion. Today all that remains is a flat plain ringed with steep walls. This makes a perfect home for lots of large animals including rhinoceros, hippopotamus, wildebeest, zebra, lions and elephants.

4. Table Mountain, South Africa

Table Mountain is a South African icon that forms a spectacular backdrop to Cape Town. The mountain is a modest 1084 m (3558 ft) high. Its unique flat top and surrounding steep cliffs form the mountain's famous shape. This is the only natural site on earth to have a constellation of stars named after it – Mensa, meaning 'the table'.

5. Victoria Falls, Zimbabwe and Zambia

The broad Zambezi River is flowing calmly when it suddenly encounters the wide edge of the Victoria Falls gorge. Then the whole river plunges 100 m (330 ft) to the bottom, throwing out plumes of mist and thunderous sounds. This wondrous spectacle inspired the native name for the falls – Mosi-oa-Tunya, which means 'smoke that thunders'.

Asia

Asia

1. Petra, Jordan

Carved right out of solid sandstone cliffs, Petra is an ancient city of tombs, temples, theatres and homes. The city is dramatically placed in a series of deep, arid gorges in southern Jordan. Many of Petra's tombs are hollowed from beautiful rainbow-coloured rock.

The main entrance to Petra is through the Siq – a narrow, twisting gorge with sheer cliff walls soaring 200 m (650 ft) straight up. The towering walls are so narrow in places they block the view of the sky.

The Nabatean people started to build Petra around 300 BC. They used an ingenious system of dams and channels to control the frequent flash floods that cut through the gorges. When an earthquake destroyed these systems in AD 363, the city soon became deserted.

Asia

1. Dead Sea, Israel and Jordan

No land on earth is lower than the shore of the Dead Sea. It lies 417 m (1368 ft) below normal sea level. The Dead Sea is nine times saltier than an ocean. This salinity makes the waters a very harsh place to live. Most marine animals and plants cannot survive in this environment. The salt also means the waters are very easy to float in – you can easily lie back and read a book!

2. Jerusalem Old City, Israel

Jerusalem is one of the world's oldest cities and has been inhabited for at least 4000 years. It is also one of the most holy places on the planet. Three faiths – Christianity, Islam and Judaism – consider it sacred. The city has been besieged and captured many times and destroyed twice.

3. Bu Tinah Island, United Arab Emirates

Bu Tinah is a tiny cluster of coral formations, low islands and lagoons in the waters of Abu Dhabi. Its highest point is only 3 m (10 ft) above sea level, making it vulnerable to rises in the ocean level. Many scientists come here to study climate change.

Bu Tinah is home to many rare types of wildlife, making it a living laboratory. It has sixteen species of coral, seagrass beds and tall mangroves. There are seabirds such as the flamingo and the osprey, the rare hawksbill turtle, and the planet's second-largest population of dugong, an endangered marine mammal.

Asia

1. Mecca, Saudi Arabia

Mecca is the holiest place in the world to Muslims. In the city's most sacred mosque is a black, cube-shaped building called the Kaaba. Muslims always face the direction of the Kaaba when praying, wherever they are in the world. The Hajj is an annual pilgrimage to Mecca. Pilgrims walk round the Kaaba seven times in an anti-clockwise direction. During the Hajj, 6 million people may visit the Kaaba in a single day.

2. Azerbaijan mud flows

Mud volcanoes look like bubbling witches' cauldrons. When erupting they belch gas and hot water into the air. There are around 1000 mud volcanoes in the world, and 400 of them are in Azerbaijan and by the Caspian Sea. They show that there are large oil and gas reserves in the area. The material they spit out comes from a mud reservoir deep under the ground. In 2001, a mud volcano surprised scientists around the world when it suddenly spat flames into the air.

1. Maldives

The Maldives is a beautiful group of 1192 low-lying coral islands. They are famed for their beaches, lagoons and wildlife. The waters abound in coral reefs, sharks, rays, turtles and 2000 species of fish. The Maldives is the lowest country on the planet with an average ground level of just 1.5 m (4 ft 11 in) above sea level. That means that one of the world's wonders may not be with us much longer as the current rate of sea level rise is a major threat.

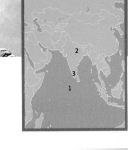

2. Ganges, India

India's Ganges River is sacred to Hindus and flows by their holiest city, Varanasi. Varanasi has about 100 ghats (stone steps leading directly into the water) where pilgrims come to wash in the holy waters. The waters here are also said to help the dead rise into heaven and people throw the cremated remains of bodies into the river. The Ganges may be holy, but it is also one of the most polluted rivers on Earth!

3. Meenakshi, India

The Meenakshi Hindu Temple in Madurai, has fourteen amazing gopurams (ornate gateways). These skyscraping towers were built in the 13th to 16th centuries. The gopurams seem to burst with life. Each one has many storeys, with thousands of brightly painted carvings of animals, gods and demons. There are at least 33 000 sculptures in the temple, but no one has managed to count them all!

1. Taj Mahal, India

The Taj Mahal is a building that never fails to knock travellers' socks off. To many, this wonder in India is the world's most beautiful structure. An emperor called Shah Jahan was so upset when his wife, Mumtaz Mahal, died in 1631 that he decided to build a spectacular mausoleum in her memory. Thousands of the best artists and craftsmen worked for 16 years on the white marble building. It has a picturesque setting on the banks of the River Yamuna, in the city of Agra.

1. Ladakh, India

Ladakh is a wild and remote region in India. It has an awesome mountain landscape and an ancient Tibetan-style culture. Perched at an altitude of 3600 m (11 800 ft), Thikse Monastery crowns a hilltop near the capital city, Leh. The monastery houses many Buddhist artworks, including statues, paintings and swords.

2. Golden Temple, India

The Golden Temple in Amritsar shines like a huge piece of jewellery in the middle of a serene blue pool. The Temple is the holiest building in the Sikh religion and 100 000 visitors bustle round its narrow walkways every day. It is adorned with beautiful marble carvings. The upper walls of the building have been covered with real gold.

3. Bagan, Myanmar

Bagan is an ancient city on the banks of the Ayeyarwady River. It was just a small settlement in the 11th century, but over the next 250 years it boomed to become the capital of an empire. The wealthy Bagan people built over 10 000 Buddhist temples, pagodas and monasteries. The famous Mongol emperor Kublai Khan attacked the Bagan empire in 1297. The city lost its power and was abandoned. But 2200 temples still stand today.

1. Komodo, Indonesia

Komodo is a volcanic island known for its brilliant white sandy beaches, blue waters and coral reefs. Komodo is also home to one of only seven beaches in the world with pink sand. Inland, the island has rugged hills and dry savannah. There are 5700 giant Komodo dragons living on the island. These are the largest lizards on earth. They have sharp teeth and will readily attack large animals.

2. Buddhist Temples, Indonesia

Borobudur is a Buddhist temple. It is an incredible structure, as high as a ten-storey building. It was built in the 9th century but later abandoned and for centuries, nobody knew where it was! It was then covered by volcanic ash and jungle and lay hidden until it was dug out in 1814 and restored to its full splendour.

3. Angkor Wat, Cambodia

Angkor Wat is the largest religious monument in the world and an architectural masterpiece. It lies deep in the Cambodian jungle on a rectangular island surrounded by a wide moat. Angkor Wat was built as a Hindu temple and capital city by King Suryavarman II in the 12th century. Eye-popping in scale, it has thousands of exquisite stone carvings.

4. Ha Long Bay, Vietnam

Ha Long Bay has thousands of rocky islands that jut sharply out of the water. These islets are topped with thick vegetation. This curious landscape was formed when water eroded limestone layers over millions of years. There are many tunnels and huge caves within the islands. The largest of these is Hang Dau Go (Wooden Stakes Cave), which has many stalactites and stalagmites.

5. Puerto Princesa, Philippines

Fancy taking a boat trip – underground? The Puerto Princesa subterranean river is one of the longest navigable underground rivers in the world. From the sea you can travel up its twisting limestone caves, passing through caverns with mighty stalactites and stalagmites.

1. Great Wall, China

The Great Wall is by far the biggest structure ever built by mankind. It was constructed in stages to protect China's northern frontier from invaders. In its heyday at the end of the Ming Dynasty (17th century), it snaked 6400 km (4000 miles) across northern China. That is the distance from London to Delhi in India! The Great Wall is 7.8 m (26 ft) high in some places and ranges from 5–10 m (16–33 ft) wide.

2. Forbidden City, China

Surrounded by a moat and high wall, the Forbidden City, in the centre of Beijing, was the home of Chinese emperors for nearly 500 years (1420–1911). No one could enter or leave the palace without the emperor's permission. It was carefully designed to show off imperial power, as well as philosophical beliefs. There are hundreds of temples, gates and ceremonial halls, decorated with carved dragons and topped with tiled roofs.

3. Potala Palace, China

Clinging to a rock high above the valley floor in Lhasa is the Potala Palace. This massive fortress-like building was once the main home of the Dalai Lama, the spiritual leader of Tibetan Buddhists. It is now a museum. The Potala Palace was built in 1645 and has more than 1000 rooms. There are also many thousands of religious shrines, statues and other artworks.

Asia

1. Hong Kong Harbour, China

Hong Kong Harbour is world-famous for its stunning skyline. Skyscrapers crowd round the bay and climb up the mountain ridges beyond. The city is a bustling melting pot of cultures with thousands of exotic restaurants and shops. The harbour is one of the busiest ports in the world. Ships chug to and fro at every hour of the day and night. Around 220 000 vessels visit Hong Kong every year.

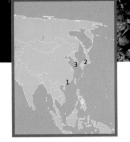

2. Kiyomizu Temple, Japan

This wonder in Kyoto is one of the world's most celebrated Buddhist sites. A temple was first built here in AD 798, and the current building was completed in 1633. It is so cleverly constructed that not a single nail is used in the entire structure. It has a shrine to a god of love, and many people come here hoping to have their romantic wishes granted.

3. Jeju Island, South Korea

Jeju is the largest island in Korea. It is famed for its white beaches, turquoise waters and beautiful waterfalls. The island was formed by an undersea volcano. Over millions of years the volcano's eruptions built it higher and higher, until it rose out of the sea and became an island.

At the heart of Jeju island is Halla-san, the tallest mountain in South Korea. This dormant volcano rises 1950 m (6398 ft) above sea level and its crowning crater is filled with a lake. The island has lots of lava tubes that once carried magma to the surface. These are now spectacular caves.

Europe

Europe

1. Stonehenge, England, UK

Stonehenge is one of the world's oldest and most mysterious archaeological wonders. Its huge megaliths (large stones) were arranged for an unknown ritual purpose by prehistoric people around 4000 years ago. The stones are up to 9 m (30 ft) high. Construction would have been an immense job without modern tools.

2. British Museum, England, UK

With 8 million artefacts, the British Museum in London has one of the world's finest collections of cultural masterpieces. There are amazing objects from almost every country on earth, including the Rosetta Stone, which scholars used to unlock the secrets of Egyptian hieroglyphics. The museum is Britain's number one tourist attraction.

3. White Cliffs of Dover, England, UK

Rising sheer from the sea, the White Cliffs of Dover seem to form a natural barrier to travellers crossing the English Channel. The cliffs are white because they are made of chalk. You can easily see them from the coast of France.

4. Edinburgh Castle, Scotland, UK

Perched on its high cliff, this citadel looks nearly unreachable. Its ancient walls can tell many stories. The Great Hall has an ornate 16th century roof that is an architectural gem. The Scottish crown jewels were lost for a century in a forgotten room but now take centre stage. When the castle's mightiest cannon last shot a ball, it landed 3.2 km (2 miles) away!

5. Eilean Donan, Scotland, UK

Eilean Donan is one of the most romantic of all Scottish castles. It sits on a tiny island in a sea loch surrounded by dramatic hills. The only way in or out is by an arched stone bridge.

6. Giant's Causeway, Northern Ireland, UK

The Giant's Causeway might look like stepping stones made by a geometrically minded sculptor, but it formed naturally when lava quickly cooled. There are around 40 000 hexagonal pillars.

7. Cliffs of Moher, Ireland

The Cliffs of Moher are where the lush farmland of Ireland drops sheer into the sea. The dizzying wall stretches for 8 km (5 miles) and stands as high as a 60-storey building above the pounding Atlantic surf.

1. Eiffel Tower, France

The Eiffel Tower is one of the most recognizable structures on earth. It is impossible to imagine Paris without this impressive example of engineering. It was built in 1889 as the entrance to a world fair in Paris. At that time it was the world's tallest man-made structure and proved so popular it was never taken down. More than 200 million people have visited the tower since it was first constructed and it is now the most visited monument in the world.

2. Palace of Versailles, France

Europe's grandest royal palace was once a simple hunting lodge. Then Louis XIV, the 'Sun King', expanded it into a glorious chateau with 2300 rooms and fountain-filled gardens. In 1682 it became the seat of the French government and a dazzling setting for state affairs.

3. Arc de Triomphe, France

The Arc de Triomphe is the world's most famous symbol of military victory. Napoleon Bonaparte ordered it to be built in 1806 after winning a vital battle. His empire was then at its peak. It also forms a hub for twelve grand Parisian avenues.

4. Alhambra, Spain

This magnificent fortress-palace was built in the 14th century by the Moors, who then ruled Spain. Its architecture is still a wonder today. Artists decorated its walls, floors and ceilings. Arcades and reflecting pools added to the beauty of the buildings.

Europe

1. Neuschwanstein Castle, Germany

Spires, turrets, gothic windows, sheer walls and a picturesque location – Neuschwanstein Castle looks like the perfect medieval castle. It was, in fact, built less than 150 years ago, in 1869 by the eccentric King Ludwig II of Bavaria, who wanted it as his ideal knightly home.

2. The Black Forest, Germany

The Black Forest (Schwarzwald in German) is a huge area of hills, valleys, rivers and forests. The Romans named it, awed by the forest's dense, sinister canopy of evergreens that blocked out much of the light. No wonder it is where Hansel and Gretel met the wicked witch!

3. Masurian Lakes, Poland

Famous for its crystal blue pools, sleepy islands and tree-lined paths, the Masurian Lakes Plateau is known as the 'Land of a Thousand Lakes'. These lakes are linked by rivers and canals to form a network of scenic waterways.

4. Kremlin, Russia

'Kremlin' means fortress, and this citadel stronghold in the heart of Moscow has several palaces and cathedrals protected behind high walls with towers. All the Russian Tsars (supreme leaders) were crowned in the main church and the Kremlin has long been the seat of power in Russia. The President of Russia now has his official home there.

5. St Basil's Cathedral, Russia

With its swirling, candy-coloured domes and towers, St Basil's Cathedral is a truly wondrous building. It was built in the 1550s by Ivan the Terrible to mark his victory over the Tartars in Central Asia. Its unique shape represents flames leaping to heaven. The cathedral's location on Red Square is at the very centre of Moscow.

6. Winter Palace, Russia

With its 1500 rooms, the vast Winter Palace in St. Petersburg was a fitting home for the Russian monarchs who at one point ruled almost one-sixth of the earth's land. But it became a symbol of a different kind in 1917, when the palace was stormed by a mob in a key moment in the Russian Revolution. Today it is part of the Hermitage, one of the largest museums in the world.

Europe

1. Colosseum, Italy

The Colosseum of Rome is fittingly named – it is the largest amphitheatre in the world. Its oval terraces once held 50 000 roaring spectators. They came to watch deadly gladiatorial fights, battle re-enactments, executions and sometimes even ordinary plays! It was inaugurated in AD 80 and now, nearly 2000 years later, it is still one of the most dramatic and historic archaeological wonders on earth.

Europe

1. Matterhorn, Italy and Switzerland
The Matterhorn is a savagely steep mountain that has fascinated (and scared) climbers for centuries. At 4478 m (14 690 ft), it is one of the highest peaks in the Alps but its distinctive pyramid shape is what makes it a unique wonder.

2. Venice Canals, Italy
How can a city have houses but no streets? When it is Venice – where the 'roadways' are actually canals. It was founded when refugees fleeing from invading Barbarians sought sanctuary on some islands in a swampy lagoon.

3. Tower of Pisa, Italy
Is this the world's wonkiest wonder? The bell tower leans because weak foundations on one side cannot support its weight. It is still a beautiful structure and part of a magnificent collection of medieval buildings.

4. Vesuvius, Italy
When the huge volcano that looms over modern day Naples erupted in AD 70, it buried the town of Pompeii under metres of ash. The town was rediscovered 1500 years later. Its excavated remains now show a fascinating snapshot of a Roman town just before catastrophe struck.

5. Acropolis, Greece

This 2400-year-old citadel is a famous symbol of the ancient Greek civilisation. The stunning Parthenon is the star attraction of the Acropolis and one of the world's greatest cultural monuments. This temple tops the skyline of Athens and was dedicated to Athena, the ancient city's favourite goddess. Its elegant columns and fine sculptures have been copied across the world.

6. Delphi, Greece

Delphi was famous in the ancient world for its oracle. This was said to be a supernatural gateway, through which priests heard prophesies from the god Apollo. Today, Delphi is a remarkable complex of historical ruins. These include a temple, an athletic stadium where games were regularly held, and a spectacular 5000-seat theatre.

7. Hagia Sophia, Turkey

Built in AD 537, Hagia Sophia was the largest cathedral in the world for 1000 years. In 1453 Sultan Mehmed captured Constantinople and turned the building into a mosque. It has been a museum since 1935. With its huge dome, marble pillars and beautiful mosaics, Hagia Sophia is a masterpiece of Byzantine architecture.

North America

1. Bay of Fundy, Canada

Where did the sea go? The tides in the Bay of Fundy are the biggest in the world – the difference between high and low water can be 17 m (55 ft). In one cycle, 100 billion tonnes of seawater floods in and out of the bay. That is greater than the flow of water in all the world's rivers combined!

2. Banff National Park, Canada

Banff National Park has one of the wildest and most wonderful landscapes on earth. Grizzly bears prowl its jagged, snow-capped mountains; wolves drink from emerald-hued lakes; glaciers unleash surging streams and flower-filled meadows offer unforgettable walks.

3. CN Tower, Canada

Stand on the top deck of the CN Tower and you can see for miles. This stunning spire rises 553 m (1815 ft), making it the tallest free-standing structure in the Western Hemisphere. If you fancy some pie in the sky, there is a revolving restaurant at the top of the tower.

4. Quebec, Canada

Quebec was one of the first European settlements in North America. Its setting on the St Lawrence River was chosen because it was good for defence. It is also very picturesque. The cobble-stoned streets of the Upper Town have history at every corner, as well as quirky shops and enticing restaurants. The city's old fortifications include a citadel and ramparts. Its most striking landmark is the Chateau Frontenac, which looks like a massive medieval castle, but is actually a hotel.

North America

1. Niagara Falls, USA and Canada

There are three cascades at Niagara Falls, and together they form one of the mightiest and most spectacular waterfalls in the world. The Horseshoe Falls are the single most powerful waterfall in North America, dropping 50 m (165 ft) in a swoop of crashing water and spray.

2. Yellowstone National Park, USA

Yellowstone National Park was the first official national park on our planet. Its stunning mountains, lakes, canyons, rivers, grasslands and forests are home to hundreds of species of animals and plants. Deep under Yellowstone is an active supervolcano, which powers the park's geothermal wonders. One of its 300 geysers is Old Faithful, which spits boiling water into the air every 90 minutes.

3. Yosemite National Park, USA

Yosemite National Park is one of the most beautiful of all wilderness parks. Its forested river valley is bounded by sheer cliffs, gnarled peaks and towering waterfalls. The most distinctive mountain is Half Dome, which has a sheer face standing 1444 m (4737 ft) above the valley floor. There are also groves of giant sequoias, the world's largest trees.

1. Grand Canyon, USA

Stand on the precipice of a 29 km (18 mile)-wide, 1.6 km (1 mile)-deep gorge in the planet's crust and your mind is sure to be boggled. Carved by the Colorado River, the Grand Canyon is a long landscape of dramatic desolation. Nearly 2 billion years of the Earth's geological history can be seen in the exposed strata.

North America

1. New York, USA

New York City has one of the world's best-known skylines thanks to the huge buildings of Manhattan. This island forms the centre of the city and it has two clusters of skyscrapers, midtown and downtown. In midtown is the Empire State Building. This was the world's tallest structure for 40 years. It is a superb example of Art Deco architecture. Downtown, the Freedom Tower, standing at 541.32 m (1776 ft), leads the crowd of giant buildings perching dramatically on the edge of the water.

1. Statue of Liberty, USA

A symbol of freedom, New York, and America – the Statue of Liberty is an icon known around the world. Since its inauguration in 1886 it has welcomed millions of ship-borne immigrants to new lives in the United States. The statue was a gift from the people of France.

2. Mount Rushmore, USA

Between 1927 and 1941 an ordinary granite mountain in the remote Black Hills of South Dakota was turned into one of the largest sculptures in history. Workers removed 450 000 tonnes of rock to create images of four famous American presidents – George Washington, Thomas Jefferson, Theodore Roosevelt and Abraham Lincoln.

3. Golden Gate Bridge, USA

San Francisco's most famous landmark was the world's tallest and widest suspension bridge when built in 1937. Although no longer a record holder, it will always be one of the most beautiful of bridges. Its towers can often be seen soaring above the swirling fog rolling in from the Pacific Ocean.

4. Chichen Itza, Mexico

Chichen Itza was one of the largest cities of the Maya people of Mexico and Central America. It is now the best preserved of the many Mayan ruins. The Maya were masters of art, architecture and mathematics. The Temple of Kukulkan is a beautifully designed step pyramid built in honour of a feathered serpent god.

5. Teotihuacan, Mexico

At Teotihuacan are the remains of an ancient city, built in the first few centuries AD. At its peak the city would have had 125 000 people and been among the largest in the world. It still has many architectural marvels, with pyramids, avenues, murals and the enormous Pyramid of the Sun, one of the grandest monuments ever erected. It is the third largest pyramid in the world.

6. El Yunque, Puerto Rico, USA

The lush jungle of El Yunque National Forest is famous for its unique flora and fauna and it was one of the first-ever protected nature reserves. More than 5 m (16.5 ft) of rain a year falls in some parts of the forest, creating majestic waterfalls and turbulent rivers. El Yunque is also famous for its native rock carvings.

South America

South America

1. Christ the Redeemer, Brazil

The mighty Christ the Redeemer is made all the more wondrous because of its dramatic location. The statue stands on the very top of a mountain above the spectacular city of Rio de Janeiro. Buildings, islands, the harbour, all lie far below the figure's feet, and he seems to be opening his arms to the whole city.

2. Rio Carnival, Brazil

Carnival in Rio is one of the world's biggest parties. Over a million tourists flock to join the 6 million locals for several days of singing, dancing and all-round merrymaking. Huge, beautifully decorated floats parade through the streets, musicians play samba music and colourful dancers put on an unforgettable show for the spectators. Carnival takes place before Lent, a traditional 40-day period of fasting.

3. Iguazu Falls, Brazil and Argentina

The Iguazu Falls form a roaring, living border between Argentina and Brazil. When the water level is low, there are around 300 islands that divide the falls into many separate cataracts. Then when the rainy season begins, up to 200 islets are totally submerged and the cascade becomes even more thunderingly impressive.

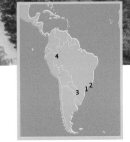

4. Amazon Rainforest

Imagine a jungle larger than Europe – you have just pictured the Amazon Rainforest. The biggest rainforest on the planet has the largest collection of plant and animal species. One in ten of all species on Earth lives in the Amazon Rainforest. At the heart of it all is the long Amazon River. This titan carries more water than the world's next seven largest rivers combined.

South America

1. Angel Falls, Venezuela

The highest waterfall in the world was found in 1933, when pilot Jimmy Angel flew over it while looking for gold. The falls lie deep in the Venezuelan jungle. The water descends 979 m (3212 ft), with a single free-fall drop of 807 m (2648 ft) – that is nineteen times higher than the drop of Niagara Falls.

2. Machu Picchu, Peru

Machu Picchu, the world's most dramatic ruin, was built by the Inca people in the 15th century, then abandoned 100 years later and lost to the jungle. It was found again in 1911. The citadel is amazing in its construction. Many of its stones are huge, and how the Inca moved and placed these enormous blocks remains a mystery.

3. Galapagos Islands

The Galapagos Islands are a natural wonderland lying off the Ecuador mainland. The young Charles Darwin visited the islands in 1835 and saw that different islands had their own kinds of birds and animals. He later realised that the different birds had slowly evolved into new versions of themselves, ones that are found nowhere else on earth. This idea became his theory of natural selection, which explained evolution and changed science forever.

The marine iguana evolved here and is the only lizard in the world that can live in the sea.

Galapagos sea lions are graceful swimmers who also love to sunbathe. They are friendly creatures that often bark playfully at visitors.

The Galapagos tortoise is the world's largest tortoise and one of the longest-lived of all creatures. A female named Harriet lived at least 170 years.

4. Easter Island, Pacific Ocean

There are 887 huge statues, or moai, on Easter Island. They stand on the hillsides with their backs to the sea. The figures were carved between 1250 and 1500 to represent ancient ancestors who the islanders believed had become gods.

63

Australasia and the Pacific Ocean

Australasia and Pacific Ocean

1. Sydney Opera House, Australia

Sydney Opera House is one of the 20th century's most distinctive buildings and a famous symbol of Australia. Its white curving roofs look like sails being blown across the waters of the harbour. The building is not just for opera. It also hosts theatre, ballet and musical performances, making it one of the busiest performing arts venues anywhere.

2. Twelve Apostles, Australia

The Twelve Apostles are rock pillars that were once part of the mainland. Over time waves and wind eroded the soft limestone of the cliffs, forming caves. These became arches, which in turn collapsed leaving rock stacks up to 45 m (148 ft) high. The sea will one day swallow these too. In fact, there are now only eight of the twelve apostles left standing.

3. Olgas, Australia

Thrusting up from the desert plain are thirty-six rusty-red domes known as the Olgas, or Kata Tjuta. They cluster close together, creating a network of deep gorges and narrow valleys. The highest point, Mount Olga, is 1066 m (3,497 ft) above the surrounding plain. The local Aboriginal people tell legends about the great snake king Wanambi who is said to live on this summit.

4. Uluru, Australia

Uluru, also known as Ayers Rock, is one of the world's largest solitary mountains. It stands like an island surrounded by a vast, flat desert plain. Uluru seems to change colours throughout the day, often glowing deep red at dawn and dusk. The rock is sacred to the local Aboriginal people. There are many springs, waterholes, rock caves and ancient paintings nearby.

5. Great Barrier Reef, Australia

The Great Barrier Reef is the world's biggest single structure made by living things. It is so big it can be seen from outer space. Made of 3000 individual coral reefs with many small islands, atolls and lagoons, the Great Barrier Reef is a playground for wildlife. There are 1500 different types of fish and 200 kinds of birds. There are also whales, dolphins and sea turtles. Millions of tourists come to see the unforgettable beauty of its fish and coral waterscapes.

1. Fiordland National Park, New Zealand

Fiordland National Park is famous for its rugged beauty. There are soaring granite peaks, high waterfalls, pristine lakes and massive fiords – long, narrow inlets of the sea with steep mountainsides. Milford Sound is the largest, longest, and deepest fiord. It is also one of the wettest places in the world. When the heavy rains come, hundreds of temporary waterfalls plunge down the cliff faces that line the fiord. Some reach 1000 m (3280 ft) in length. Smaller falls may never reach the bottom of the sound, drifting away as spray in the wind.

2. Rotorua, New Zealand

Rotorua is one of the world's most amazing geothermal wonderlands. It has over a thousand geothermal features. Geysers spurt skywards, mud baths bubble like cauldrons, hot springs steam and boil, mineral pools sparkle in rainbow colours. The Lady Knox Geyser erupts at 10:15 am each day, sometimes soaring up to 30 m (98 ft) in the air.

3. Bora Bora, French Polynesia

Is this the most beautiful island in the world? At the heart of Bora Bora is an extinct volcano, rising in jagged steps to 727 m (2385 ft). This crumbling mountain is covered with lush vegetation and surrounded by a tropical emerald-turquoise lagoon. Ringing the lagoon are coral islands, strung together by reefs like pearls on a necklace.

4. Hawai'i Volcanoes National Park

Hawai'i Volcanoes National Park is home to Mauna Loa and Kilauea, two of the most active and exciting volcanoes in the world. Mauna Loa is the largest volcano on earth. It started erupting on the seabed 700 000 years ago and poked out of the ocean to become an island 300 000 years later. Kilauea is the most active of Hawai'i's five volcanoes. Its latest eruption started in 1983 and is still going strong.

Index

Acknowledgements

Image credits

All images credited unless unknown. Pages with multiple images are acknowledged from top to bottom

Cover Images

Sphinx : Pius Lee/Shutterstock.com
Camel: Lenar Musin/Shutterstock.com
Pyramids: sculpies/Shutterstock.com

Main Images

P4–5 Images in public domain
P6–7 © sculpies/Shutterstock.com
P8–9 © Dmussman/Shutterstock.com
P10 © Michele Alfieri/Shutterstock.com, © Lenar Musin/Shutterstock.com, © WitR/Shutterstock.com
P11 © Bjorn Hoglund/Shutterstock.com, © Francois Gagnon/Shutterstock.com
P12 © Graeme Shannon/ Shutterstock.com, © AndreAnita/Shutterstock.com, © StephanScherhag/Shutterstock.com
P13 © michaeljung/Shutterstock.com, © wolfso/Shutterstock.com
P14–15 © Hung Chung Chih/ Shutterstock.com
P16 © Waj/Shutterstock.com
P17 © thanomphong/Shutterstock.com, © Aleksandar Todorovic/Shutterstock.com
P18 © vvoe/Shutterstock.com, © David Rafael Moulis/Shutterstock.com
P19 Aenaon/wikipedia
P20 © Zurijeta/Shutterstock.com
P21 © Jan Krcmar/Shutterstock.com, © Tonis Valing/Shutterstock.com
P22 © Lorenzo Mondo/Shutterstock.com
P23 © turtix/Shutterstock.com, © Rafal Gaweda/Shutterstock.com
P24–25 © alfredolon/Shutterstock.com
P26 © littleworrmy/Shutterstock.com, © David Evison/Shutterstock.com
P27 © Chantal de Bruijne/ Shutterstock.com

P28 © Rafal Gaweda/Shutterstock.com, © Pius Lee/Shutterstock.com, © Pigprox/Shutterstock.com
P29 © Tom Roche/Shutterstock.com, © PhotoRoman/Shutterstock.com, © audioscience/Shutterstock.com
P30 © Hung Chung Chih/ Shutterstock.com
P31 © 06photo/Shutterstock.com, © qian/Shutterstock.com
P32 © leungchopan/Shutterstock.com
P33 © Martin Mette/Shutterstock.com, © Maxim Tupikov/Shutterstock.com, © Maxim Tupikov/Shutterstock.com
P34–35 © S.Borisov/Shutterstock.com
P36 © Matthew Jacques/ Shutterstock.com, © jennyt/Shutterstock.com, © Tony Taylor stock/Shutterstock.com

P37 © Bertl123/Shutterstock.com, © Gudmund/Shutterstock.com, © Joe Gough/Shutterstock.com, © Agnieszka Guzowska/Shutterstock.com
P38 © TanArt/Shutterstock.com
P39 © Pecold/Shutterstock.com, © Samot/Shutterstock.com, © Dan Breckwoldt/Shutterstock.com
P40 © Eremeev/Shutterstock.com, © PRILL/Shutterstock.com, © Patryk Kosmider/Shutterstock.com
P41 © Kingan/Shutterstock.com, © Marcos81/Shutterstock.com, © rasskazov/Shutterstock.com
P42–43 © Alexandra Lande/ Shutterstock.com
P44 © pinggr/Shutterstock.com, © Pecold/Shutterstock.com, © Ivan Smuk/Shutterstock.com, © Danilo Ascione/Shutterstock.com
P45 © S.Borisov/Shutterstock.com, © Todd Kreykes/Shutterstock.com, © Tatiana Popova/Shutterstock.com
P46–47 © Ami Parikh/Shutterstock.com
P48 © GVictoria/Shutterstock.com, © Protasov AN/Shutterstock.com
P49 © Elena Elisseeva/Shutterstock.com,

© Suchan/Shutterstock.com
P50 © R Rusak/Shutterstock.com
P51 © Lorcel/Shutterstock.com, © an Schreiber/Shutterstock.com
P52-53 © Diana Beato/Shutterstock.com
P54–55 © Donald R. Swartz/ Shutterstock.com
P56 © gracious_tiger/Shutterstock.com, © Jochen Lambrechts/Shutterstock.com, © Click Images/Shutterstock.com
P57 © Borys Tronko/Shutterstock.com, © f9photos/Shutterstock.com, © Jason Patrick Ross/Shutterstock.com
P58–59 © Leanne Vorrias/ Shutterstock.com
P60 © Mark Schwettmann/ Shutterstock.com, © Leanne Vorrias/Shutterstock.com, © Bill Ramsden/Shutterstock.com
P61 © Dr. Morley Read/Shutterstock.com
P62 © Vadim Petrakov/Shutterstock.com, © my Nichole Harris/Shutterstock.com
P63 © Dmitry Saparov/Shutterstock.com, © Natursports/Shutterstock.com, © Stacy Funderburke/Shutterstock.com
© Kayla A/Shutterstock.com
© Rachel Sanderoff/Shutterstock.com
P64–65 © Pete Niesen/Shutterstock.com
P66 © Neale Cousland/ Shutterstock.com, © Markus Gann/Shutterstock.com, © Andy Clarke/Shutterstock.com

P67 © Stanislav Fosenbauer/ Shutterstock.com, © JonMilnes/Shutterstock.com
P68 © Graeme Knox/Shutterstock.com, © teeshirt/Shutterstock.com
P69 © Christian Wilkinson/ Shutterstock.com, © Lijuan Guo/Shutterstock.com, © Bryan Busovicki/Shutterstock.com

Title strip images

P6–7 © sculpies/Shutterstock.com
P10–11 © Lenar Musin//Shutterstock.com

P12–13 © Graeme Shannon/ Shutterstock.com
P16–17 © Aleksandar Todorovic/ Shutterstock.com
P18–19 © vvoe/Shutterstock.com
P20–21 © Tonis Valing/Shutterstock.com
P22–23 © Rafal Gaweda/ Shutterstock.com
P24–25 © Luciano Mortula/ Shutterstock.com
P26–27 © marcovarro/ Shutterstock.com
P28–29 © Rafal Gaweda/ Shutterstock.com
P30–31 © qian/Shutterstock.com
P32–33 © Maxim Tupikov/ Shutterstock.com
P36–37 © Tony Taylor stock/ Shutterstock.com
P38–39 © Dan Breckwoldt/ Shutterstock.com
P40–41 ©PRILL/Shutterstock.com
P42–43 © Alexandra Lande/ Shutterstock.com
P44–45 © Ivan Smuk/Shutterstock.com
P48–49 © Protasov AN/Shutterstock.com
P50–51 © R Rusak/Shutterstock.com
P52–53 © Diana Beato/Shutterstock.com
P54–55 © Donald R. Swartz/ Shutterstock.com
P56–57 © Click Images/ Shutterstock.com
P60–61 © Dr. Morley Read/ Shutterstock.com
P62–63 © Dmitry Saparov/ Shutterstock.com
P66–67 © JonMilnes/Shutterstock.com
P68–69 © Christian Wilkinson/ Shutterstock.com

Text

Main text: Richard Happer